THE CHOICE IS YOURS.

THAT IS THE CORE PHILOSOPHY OF THE MINDFUL LIFE PROGRAM CREATED BY JAE ELLARD. The choice is yours to start anywhere at any point in your life to create more awareness around the choices you make each day that either support or sabotage your desired outcome to create meaningful engagement and sustainable balance between the interconnected (and many times blurry) roles, relationships and responsibilities that make up your life.

The Mindful Life program includes four conversations to generate reflection, awareness, and action.

Stop & Think: Creating New Awareness is about the choices you have and understanding the impact of the choices you make.

Stop & See: Developing Intentional Habits is about your ability to consciously choose to create habits that support your definitions of balance and success.

Stop & Listen: Practicing Presence is about working with your choices to create deeper engagement with self, others and your environment.

Beyond Tips & Tricks: Mindful Management is about leading groups to take accountability for making and accepting choices.

AWARENESS

GOOD NEWS

You don't have to reinvent your life, quit your job, or go to therapy to feel more in balance. Rather, the key to balance lies within cultivating awareness — awareness around your values, words, and actions. It's only natural if the sarcastic voice within just said, "Oh, is that all?"

Cultivating awareness is no small task; it takes an open attitude and a willingness to create a future that is different from the past. You'll be happy to know that it's not rocket science either.

IT'S EASY TO MAKE YOUR LACK OF BALANCE YOUR MANAGER'S FAULT, YOUR MANAGER'S MANAGER'S FAULT, YOUR COWORKERS' FAULT, OR EVEN YOUR PARTNER'S FAULT. It's possible that shifting the way you work does not even feel realistic or possible. Perhaps you fear that management might perceive you as an underperformer or, worse, incompetent if you were to appear to have a life that is balanced.

Maybe you fear that you might be seen as weak if you say no to a stretch assignment and worse, your colleagues might compete harder against you for promotion opportunities.

THIS IS ALL POSSIBLE

By taking personal accountability for your level of work-life balance, you better define all your relationships, including the one with the company. As with any relationship, clarity and communication ensure balance and sustainable success, and the path to clarity and communication starts with awareness.

AWARENESS IS **THE ABILITY TO** SEE THE WORLD **AND HOW** YOU SHOW UP IN IT.

MORE GOOD NEWS

Awareness is a skill, a skill that can be learned.

Just like learning to become a good listener or presenter, you were taught and you practiced (and probably still do practice) keeping your skills sharp. It's the same for awareness. First you learn, and then you practice; then one day it's as natural as walking.

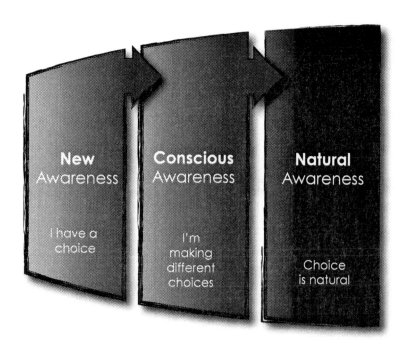

SO WHAT DOES AWARENESS REALLY MEAN?

Awareness, or personal awareness, is data; it's knowledge about you. As with any type of knowledge, knowledge is power — awareness is power. The skill of awareness can become your secret personal power to design a life made up of the type of balance that works for you at whatever stage of life you are in.

The Mindful Life program is based on the Awareness Framework methodology to build your awareness skills. The framework will help identify blocking behaviors and create opportunities to improve engagement with the outcome to improve communication, connection, and balance. The framework is designed to empower you to develop awareness around your behavior, identify the impact of your behavior, and seek sustainable results.

It's widely known that behavior has an impact and that there is a result, whether intentional or unintentional, related to the behavior. When people choose to or are empowered to become more aware of their behavior (hence the name), they are able to be more accountable in their roles and to their teams, more authentic in their communication, and more awake in their environment (both literally and figuratively.) The impact to the team and the individual is a shift in the ability to be more innovative and more productive on multiple levels. The result is sustainable success for both the organization and individual.

THE AWARENESS FRAMEWORK

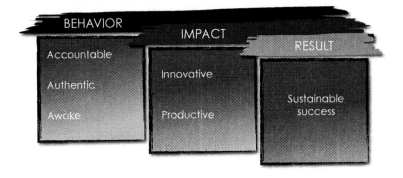

WHAT DOES BALANCE MEAN?

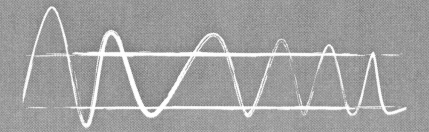

No two people share the same idea or have the same need for balance, because **BALANCE IS SOMETHING DIFFERENT TO EVERYONE.** Moreover, the meaning of balance changes over time for each person as one's values in life shift with age and through different life experiences. For example, a single, 27-year-old woman most likely does not have the same idea of balance as a 34-year-old father of two, and a married working mother doesn't have the same idea of balance as a single dad. A teenager will be different from a grandparent, and a stay-at-home parent will be different from a working parent.

BALANCE IS PERSONAL, AND EACH PERSON HAS HIS OR HER OWN IDEA OF WHAT IS ACCEPTABLE, TOLERABLE, AND COMFORTABLE. It is very important to remember that there is no right or wrong idea of balance and that your need for balance will change as your life circumstances change.

THINK

What does balance mean to YOU?

What would having this type of balance in your life make POSSIBLE?

What do you NEED to have this type of balance?

DO

Answer the questions for yourself.

Share the questions with your team and family.

BEHAVIOR

"I'VE LEARNED THAT PEOPLE WILL FORGET WHAT YOU SAID, PEOPLE WILL FORGET WHAT YOU DID, BUT PEOPLE WILL NEVER FORGET HOW YOU MADE THEM FEEL."

— Maya Angelou

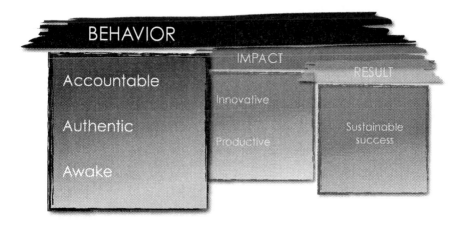

BEHAVIOR

Accountable

Authentic

Awake

IMPACT

Innovative

Productive

RESULT

Sustainable success

Can you recall how your favorite teacher made you feel? How did your parents make you feel as a child? What about your first manager or your current manager? If you are a manager, how do you think you make your directs feel?

Like Newton's third law of motion says, whether intentional or unintentional, your behavior shows up as actions and those actions cause a feeling, reaction or emotional response.

When people choose to or are empowered to become more aware of their behavior (actions and words), they are able to be more ACCOUNTABLE, AUTHENTIC, and AWAKE in their environments in and outside of work.

Countless research has shown that people who have greater work-life balance are more likely to experience better overall health and lower stress levels and to have a more positive impact on their job. Lack of balance might manifest itself in the following ways:

LACK OF ENGAGEMENT

LOW PRODUCTIVITY

HIGH STRESS (MENTAL AND PHYSICAL)

POOR WORK PERFORMANCE

DIVIDED LOYALTIES

MISSED TIME WITH FRIENDS AND FAMILY

FEELINGS OF GUILT

LOW ENERGY

When it comes to cultivating awareness around behavior, there are three layers to be aware of:

KNOW YOURSELF

EXPRESS YOURSELF

SEE YOURSELF

KNOW YOURSELF

WHAT MAKES YOU FEEL OUT OF BALANCE?

Odds are strong that most of the time, when you are feeling out of balance it is because of values. Your values may feel threatened, or you have gotten away from them, or have not communicated them or set boundaries to protect them. Values represent some of your most deeply held beliefs, which guide your behaviors and decision making. Your values reflect your highest priorities and motivators. They subconsciously guide your life. We make choices about where we work, whom we marry/date, and what we do with our free time largely based on our values.

THINK

What do you value?

How do you spend your money and your time?

In what areas are your ACTIONS (e.g., calendar and checkbook) in or out of alignment with your VALUES?

VALUE WORDS: love, family, friendship, faith, health, wealth, community, compassion, environment, integrity, honesty, freedom, creativity, art, adventure, diversity, accountability, accomplishment, efficiency, calm, loyalty, learning, leadership, innovation, fairness, change, equality, knowledge, cleanliness, flexibility, fun, generosity, orderliness, gratitude, perfection, cooperation, personal growth, perseverance, pleasure, joy, health and well-being, courage, culture, success, thinking, time/timelines, protection, reason, regularity, respect (of self and others), trust, privacy, nature, genius, courtesy, peace, lifestyle . . .

DO

Answer the questions for yourself.

Share the questions with your team and family.

Aligning values and actions is the same as learning a new skill, and it can be very difficult at first. Give yourself permission to admit/acknowledge if your values have changed or to accept that they are out of alignment with your current behavior.

THE IMPORTANT PART IS TO BE AWARE OF HOW YOUR VALUES AND YOUR ACTIONS ALIGN SO YOU CAN MOVE TOWARD CREATING A PLAN FOR IMPROVED BALANCE.

If you discovered a behavior or habit you want to try and alter, know that it will take time for the new behavior to become part of your routine. LEARNING HOW TO PUSH BACK AND SAY NO TO THINGS (ACTIONS) THAT DON'T ALIGN TO YOUR IDENTIFIED VALUES IS THE FIRST STEP TO CHANGING YOUR BEHAVIOR.

Most personal imbalance occurs when people spend time, money, or energy (or all three) on actions that don't align with their values. Owning your no's can be hard at first, but it will get easier if how your express yourself is in alignment with your values and actions.

EXPRESS YOURSELF

The hard work you've done identifying and aligning your values and actions will be meaningless if what you are communicating contradicts your actions. **COMMUNICATION IS JUST AS MUCH ABOUT YOUR ACTIONS AS IT IS ABOUT YOUR WORDS.** Nonverbal communication accounts for 80 percent of all communication, so living your values, as well as stating them, speaks volumes to those in your life.

We all know a person who says one thing, then does the exact opposite. It can be maddening; at the very least, it's confusing. **IT'S REASONABLE TO ASSUME THAT THE PERSON WHO SAYS ONE THING AND DOES ANOTHER IS OUT OF ALIGNMENT WITH HIS/HER VALUES.**

Expressing your values with the important people in your professional and personal life will create another layer of balance in the amount of understanding and support you're receiving around why you are doing what you are doing. (People cannot support what they don't know needs to be supported.)

It doesn't mean you have to share everything with everyone (unless you want to). **EXPRESSING YOURSELF MEANS COMMUNICATING WITH OTHERS WHAT'S IMPORTANT TO YOU.** Clear expression and communication will set you up for greater success at achieving a more balanced lifestyle.

Many times we knock ourselves off balance by saying things we don't mean, or agreeing to things that we have no intention of doing.

THIS IS CALLED HEDGING, AND IT OFTEN CONSISTS OF USING PHRASES LIKE "I DON'T KNOW," "MAYBE," AND "WE'LL SEE," WHEN YOU KNOW YOUR ANSWER BUT HAVE SOME FEAR AROUND STATING YOUR TRUE INTENTION.

(It's okay — we have ALL done this, so go easy on yourself here.) When you hedge, you not only create more work for yourself in the long run to set the record straight, you cause stress for yourself in having to deal with the situation longer than necessary. Not to mention, you create an expectation on you from another person that isn't necessary.

ANOTHER WAY WE EXPRESS OURSELVES IS BY COMPLAINING, OR IN SOME CASES WITHHOLDING OUR COMPLAINTS. WE ALL LOVE TO COMPLAIN, ESPECIALLY WHEN WE ARE FEELING OUT OF BALANCE. The funny thing about complaining is, many people are not clear on what it is they are actually complaining about, and many people confuse complaining with criticizing.

A complaint is an expression of your feelings of displeasure.

A criticism is rooted in judgment of the actions, values, or work of others.

Odds are you're complaining about something because you are feeling that a value of yours has been threatened or compromised in some way. (It always goes back to values.) IT'S POSSIBLE THAT SOMETIMES YOUR FEELINGS OF DISPLEASURE COME OUT AS CRITICISM, MEANING THAT IT'S EASY TO MAKE THE DISPLEASURE YOU ARE FEELING SOMEONE ELSE'S FAULT — for example, blaming your boss for you having to stay late or your partner for you not having the time to go to the gym. And when you withhold the complaint, you make it nearly impossible for you, or anyone else, to ever resolve the displeasure you are experiencing.

Be brutally honest with yourself and determine what it is you are really complaining about. Get clear on the root problem and what value is being threatened. Is it that your manager really expects you to work late — or are you struggling with managing your time at the office? Is it really that you need additional resources to help you do the job — or do you need to learn new skills to do your job well? Is it that your team is horrible — or are you in the wrong role on your team?

After you let go of criticism, you can become aware of the way you complain and how your complaints come across. Complaints fall into four categories: I just want to ruminate, I want someone to care, I don't want to talk about it, or I want something different and here's how to do it a new way.

Frivolous

Attention

Withholding

Action

Stop complaining about what is not working. Trust that everyone is already aware (probably painfully aware) of the issues — they want to hear a solution for solving the complaint.

It is easy to hear the difference in others when they complain **TO YOU**; the challenging part is listening to the voice in your head when you complain **TO OTHERS**. Learn to be aware of with whom you are sharing what type of complaint. (Hint: Your manager probably doesn't want to hear you ruminate.)

When it comes to communication, the key to creating more balance is to be authentic — say what you mean and mean what you say. Not doing so can create false expectations in the person or people you are communicating with and needlessly create stressful situations.

THINK

How often do you use hedging words?

How often do you complain?

Do you know what you are really complaining about?

DO

Answer the questions for yourself.

Share the questions with your team and family.

SEE YOURSELF

HOW DO OTHERS SEE YOU?

There are many variations on the saying that "reality is perception and perception is reality." **WHEN IT COMES TO UNDERSTANDING BALANCE — BOTH YOURS AND THE TEAM YOU ARE PART OF — PERCEPTION IS INDEED REALITY.** Cultivating personal awareness is about seeing inside you to understand your values and actions (know yourself and express yourself), as well as having the external awareness around how your actions and words are perceived by others.

Do people see you as the person who never has any time for anything? Are you the person who is in back-to-back meetings most every day, with your cell phone at your side most nights? Are your weekends spent trying to catch up or dig out? Are you late to every meeting because every meeting you are in runs over? Do you ever hear yourself at home say to your loved ones, "Just a few more minutes"?

Like it or not, other people are aware of your behavior (actions and words), especially when it comes to balance (their perception of your balance), and this can have an impact on relationships as well as productivity. **HOW WE MANAGE OUR TIME SPEAKS VOLUMES ABOUT HOW OTHERS PERCEIVE US AND HOW WE SHOW UP IN OUR ENVIRONMENTS.**

The results of many workplace studies show that the majority of employees feel that they do not have enough time for the important aspects of their personal lives and that their jobs often deprive them of time with loved ones, to the detriment of their health, well-being, and productivity.

It's common for people to feel they would have better work-life balance if they had more time. That might be true in some cases; however, odds are strong that if they got more time, it would soon be filled. IT'S NOT ABOUT HAVING MORE TIME, IT'S ABOUT HOW YOU USE THE TIME YOU HAVE.

The good news is that time management is one of the most actionable areas of bringing balance to your life. There are hundreds of books on the market about time management and improving productivity that contain tips about managing Outlook, planning meetings, and structuring your day, all of which can be an invaluable resource to helping you feel in balance. THE PURPOSE OF THIS CONVERSATION IS TO HELP YOU UNDERSTAND WHY YOU SPEND YOUR TIME THE WAY YOU DO.

HOW DO YOU GET THINGS DONE?

This is a very different question than do you function with your inbox at zero and are your meetings color-coded in Outlook. This is about analyzing how you spend your time and learning to be strategic with where you put your energy. Consider how you spend your average day in terms of the order and process with which you do things: **ARE YOU DOING IT THAT WAY BECAUSE IT IS THE BEST USE OF YOUR TIME, OR BECAUSE YOU'VE ALWAYS DONE IT THAT WAY? ARE YOU REALLY THINKING ABOUT WHY YOU ARE DOING WHAT YOU ARE DOING?**

Consider where and when you run errands: How many days a week do you go to the food market? How many calendars do you manage? If you have children, what is your childcare plan and how much do the children help around the house? If the kids are not helping around the house, consider why not.

Go beyond thinking about how many hours per week you spend at work; think about your commute time, the time you spend on the internet, and time spent running around town. **IS IT POSSIBLE TO MAKE BETTER USE OF YOUR TIME BY SHIFTING HOW AND WHEN YOU ARE DOING WHAT YOU ARE DOING?**

Another powerful way to use your time wisely is by making the choice to be in the moment you are in and do away with multitasking.

Several research studies have shown that multitasking is a waste of time because it divides attention, therefore decreasing the quality of work and quality of experience. If you stop trying to do two (or more) things at once, odds are you might enjoy what you are doing more and have fewer tasks you need to follow up on later. IT'S POSSIBLE THAT YOU CAN INCREASE THE LEVEL OF BALANCE IN YOUR LIFE SIMPLY BY DOING ONE THING AT A TIME.

If the people in your environments perceive you to be more connected in the moment you are in and more engaged on every level, it's possible you will experience a shift in balance, leading to deeper relationships.

THINK

How do you spend the time you have?

Why do you do the things you do in the order you do them in?

What action robs you of the most time?

DO

Answer the questions for yourself.

Share the questions with your team and family.

QUESTIONS TO CONSIDER

Do you consider yourself to be authentic in your communication?

How do you think others perceive your level of work-life balance?

How do you think your actions make other people feel?

Are you present in all of your environments?

What do you complain about the most?

Do those around you know what is most important to you?

Are you able to say no when necessary to protect or honor your values?

PRACTICE SUGGESTIONS

Be open to seeing how your behavior (actions and words)
is in or out of alignment with your values.

Listen to what you say (and write in emails) — is it authentic and
does it correlate to your values?

Understand the values behind your complaints.

Hear yourself — are you complaining just to complain,
or do you really want change?

Look for where you hedge in conversation.

IMPACT

"A LIFE IS NOT IMPORTANT EXCEPT IN THE IMPACT IT HAS ON OTHER LIVES."

— Jackie Robinson, first African-American Major League Baseball player

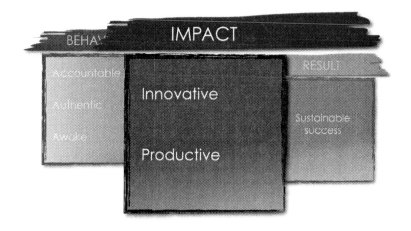

IMPACT

BEHAV...

Accountable

Authentic

Awake

Innovative

Productive

RESULT

Sustainable success

NEVER UNDERESTIMATE THE IMPACT YOU HAVE ON OTHER PEOPLE.

It is almost impossible to fully understand how your behavior (actions and words) has impacted others in the span of your life. Think for a moment about someone who has impacted you greatly in your life. Do they even know it? Do you think they did it on purpose?

Behavior (actions and words) has an impact, and there is a result, whether intentional or unintentional, related to the behavior. THE IMPACT YOUR AND OTHERS' BEHAVIOR HAS ON THE TEAM AND ORGANIZATION CAN SHIFT THE TEAM'S ABILITY TO BE MORE (OR LESS) INNOVATIVE AND PRODUCTIVE ON MULTIPLE LEVELS.

Work-life balance is not a new issue. Leaders, managers, human resource professionals, and employees have been grappling with the impact of this issue for almost 40 years. Over the coming decade, work-life balance will be one of the most important issues that executives and human resource professionals will be expected to manage. Companies that ignore the issue jeopardize losing their competitive edge and their ability to attract top talent, and also risk having higher healthcare costs and lower employee morale and productivity. The impact of the situation costs the United States an estimated $150 billion per year in absenteeism, reduced productivity, monetary compensation, insurance premiums, and medical expenses related to stress, and an estimated €20 billion in the European Union.

When employees (and their behaviors) are out of balance, there are many impacts, both direct and indirect, to the organization and the individual.

ORGANIZATIONAL IMPACT

DIRECT: occasional absence, short-term disability, long-term disability, overtime, salaries for replacement staff, training costs for replacement staff, medication costs

INDIRECT: reduced productivity, increased turnover, deterioration of work atmosphere, unhappy workers, and presenteeism. (Presenteeism refers to a condition in which an individual who suffers from a health problem, either mental or physical, remains at work, even though his or her efficiency and performance are reduced.)

INDIVIDUAL IMPACT

DIRECT: lack of engagement, low productivity, high stress (mental and physical), poor work performance, divided loyalties, missed time with friends and family, feelings of guilt

INDIRECT: physical impact of stress on body, low energy, impact to quality of relationships with friends and family, mental health issues

SO WHAT IS HAPPENING?

Why do we stay out of balance when we know what we are doing is not working? Some of the answers can be found in the field of neuroscience, which studies interactions of the brain with its environment. There are many theories that exist that say our actions are linked with our senses: smell, taste, feel/touch, seeing, and hearing, including the internal conversations we hear in our head. **IN OTHER WORDS, OUR ACTIONS (BEHAVIOR AND WORDS) ARE LINKED WITH OUR SENSES AND OUR INTERNAL DIALOGUE.** It is possible that we continue to repeat the past because we experience the same internal conversations and related sensory experiences over and over again without change or interruption to the pattern or perception. When we repeat the same cycles over and over, it makes it difficult for innovation to thrive.

HARNESSING THE POWER OF YOUR IMPACT IS AS SIMPLE AS CHANGING THE DIALOGUE IN YOUR HEAD (oh, is that all?). If you alter the dialogue in your head, your actions will begin to change as well. WHEN YOU SHIFT HOW YOU EXPERIENCE AND THINK ABOUT YOUR PERSONAL OR PROFESSIONAL WORLDS, THE BEHAVIOR OF OTHERS AROUND YOU WILL ALSO EXPERIENCE A SHIFT. It's the same principle as "a smile is contagious." You can change what you are experiencing by changing the conversations you have with yourself.

How you see the world, and the conversations you have in your head about it, make up how you relate to the world. This can be referred to as your state of being.

WHEN IT COMES TO BALANCE, THERE ARE TWO CHOICES FOR BEING.

DISEMPOWERED

This state of being is one in which you feel overstressed and as if there is never enough time. Your life might feel like a house of cards — if one card falls, the house will crumble. You might feel anxious, as though you have to defend yourself and/or the status of your work at all times. You tend to feel as if it's all yours to lose and resources and support are scarce; you operate from a place of fear. You will most likely approach interactions with others from this perception or way of being. Most people facing a crisis of work-life balance feel disempowered and are unable to be innovative in how they perform and navigate their life.

EMPOWERED

This state of being is a feeling of having a purpose. You most likely have a feeling of clear direction and connectedness to the goings-on around you. You likely feel energized and absorbed in what you are doing and feel the value of achieving what you are committed to. IF YOU ARE FUNCTIONING IN THIS STATE, YOU FEEL EMPOWERED, AS THOUGH YOU HAVE SOMETHING (OR EVERYTHING) TO GAIN: IT IS A PLACE OF ABUNDANCE. You will most likely approach interactions with others from this perception or way of being. Most people who live a balanced lifestyle feel empowered and are able to be innovative in how they perform and navigate life.

THINK

Do you operate from an empowered or disempowered state of being?

What state of being is more common among your teammates?

What can you do to shift the state of being?

DO

Answer the questions for yourself.

Share the questions with your team and family.

PHYSIOLOGICAL IMPACT: STRESS

There is a physiological component to balance in how empowered and disempowered states of being impact your body in the form of stress. Just like balance, stress means different things to different people, and stress impacts each person differently. Many scientific disciplines have proven that when a body and/or brain are under stress, productivity is greatly affected on many levels. IF YOU OR YOUR TEAM OPERATES FROM A DISEMPOWERED STATE OF BEING, NOT ONLY WILL THEIR ABILITY TO INNOVATE BE DIMINISHED, SO WILL THEIR PRODUCTIVITY.

Researchers know that just like balance, stress means different things to different people. What is stressful to you might not be stressful to your manager, coworkers, friends, or spouse. IT IS IMPORTANT TO REMEMBER THAT WHEN IT COMES TO DEFINING STRESS, EVERYBODY HAS THEIR OWN IDEA OF WHAT IS ACCEPTABLE, TOLERABLE, AND COMFORTABLE.

Stress is an important part of the natural world, aiding the natural selection and development of species. Simply put, the better species adapt to stress, the greater their odds of thriving and surviving. That said, the events that stressed us out as cave people are very different from the events that cause us stress in the modern world. Being able to cope with and navigate the stress of the modern world impacts not only our ability to thrive as a species, but also the quality of the life we live.

When we face danger, such as being chased by a wild animal, the body secretes into the bloodstream epinephrine ("adrenaline"), norepinephrine, and cortisol (also known as the stress hormone) to initiate the body's "fight or flight" response. This combination causes a quick burst of energy for survival reasons, heightened memory functions, a burst of increased immunity, and lower sensitivity to pain (not to mention sweaty palms and a racing heart).

After an injection of cortisol and adrenaline into the bloodstream, it's important that the body and brain move to a relaxation response so hormone levels can return to normal. IF THE BODY AND BRAIN DO NOT HAVE THE CHANCE TO RELAX, THE RESULT IS A CHRONIC STRESS STATE, WHICH CAN DAMAGE COGNITIVE FUNCTION INCLUDING MEMORY, EXECUTIVE FUNCTION, AND MOTOR SKILLS, ALL SKILLS THAT HELP YOU BE MORE PRODUCTIVE. Chronic stress can disrupt the immune system, sleep patterns, digestion, growth, and even reproduction — making the impact on production very literal indeed.

Research says it takes 40 to 60 minutes for cortisol levels to return to baseline and for body functioning to return to a normal state. When problems persist, the brain perceives stress; even if there is no physical threat, your body remains stressed, and sustained stress can lead to serious health issues. Serious stress-related health issues include, but are not limited to, high blood pressure, heart disease, anxiety, depression, weight gain, irritable bowel syndrome, ulcers, decreased immunity, and sleep problems.

Lots of things can cause stress. Learning the difference between healthy, short-lived stress versus chronic (prolonged) stress can better help you plan for and manage stressful situations.

The most common big stress triggers in life include moving, switching jobs, divorce, and death. Common situations that can lead to chronic stress states include unhealthy relationships, overcommitting oneself, dysfunctional work teams, and unrealistic expectations of self and others.

THINK

What stresses you out? (Is it a person, a place, or a situation?)

How do these situations make your body and mind feel? (Consider any patterns you might have developed over time.)

What do you do to take care of yourself when you are feeling stressed?

DO

Answer the questions for yourself.

Share the questions with your team and family.

QUESTIONS TO CONSIDER

What impact is your behavior (actions and words) having on people in your life in and outside of work?

Is the dialogue in your head coming from an empowered or disempowered state of being?

Do you do enough to reduce the impact stress has on your body?

Do others' states of being impact how you feel? Is it a positive or negative impact?

PRACTICE SUGGESTIONS

Listen closely to the voice in your head.

Be open to shifting to a more empowered state of being.

Consider how you could be more productive just by shifting the conversation in your head.

Get clear on the people, places, and situations that cause you stress.

Look for physical trends in how stress manifests within your body.

RESULT

"SUCCESS IS DEPENDENT ON EFFORT."

— Sophocles, ancient Greek playwright

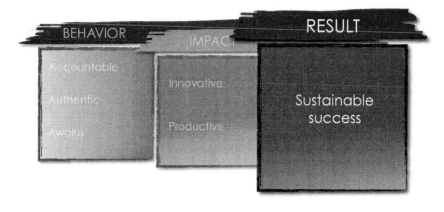

The result of building your awareness skills is power —
personal power for you to design a life made up of the type of
balance that is sustainable for years, decades to come. When
practiced often, awareness becomes a lifestyle; a way of being
that allows you to have the type of personal freedom you desire
in any given situation.

SUSTAINABILITY IS A RESULT OF INDIVIDUALS WHO ARE EMPOWERED
TO LIVE A LIFE THAT CREATES THE TIME AND BOUNDARIES TO HONOR
THEIR VALUES.

Before we can move to construct a plan to support balance, it's
important to establish the boundaries you are going to set to
uphold your plan.

As previously discussed, odds are strong that when you are feeling out of balance, it has to do with values. Sometimes it's because your values may feel threatened, or you have gotten away from them, and a lot of the time it is has to do with the boundaries you set (or don't set) to protect and honor your values.

On a very simple level, boundaries teach other people what your values are and how to treat you. Communicating your boundaries helps those in your life to be clear about what your limits are and how far you are willing to go (or not go) in certain situations and circumstances. HEALTHY WORKPLACE BOUNDARIES KEEP YOU CLEAR ON YOUR BUSINESS PURPOSE, PRIORITIES, AND TIME MANAGEMENT.

Boundaries are tricky, because you cannot see, smell, taste, or touch a boundary, but you know when it has been crossed, and you know when you are in a relationship with someone at work who is crossing the line. A good indication someone has crossed the line with you is that you might find yourself pretending that you didn't actually see what you saw or hear what you heard in order to avoid conflict or confrontation.

WHAT DO YOU NEED?

Before you can set and maintain workplace boundaries that will enable you to be more innovative and productive, it's important to get clear about your own boundaries. As with identifying your values, identifying your boundaries can be a bit difficult if you are not used to thinking about them, or perhaps have never thought about them in this way before. IDENTIFYING HEALTHY WORKPLACE BOUNDARIES IS A KEY ELEMENT TO ACHIEVING SUSTAINABLE SUCCESS IN LIVING A MORE BALANCED LIFE.

Another element of defining workplace boundaries is to build your awareness for when a boundary has been violated. For example, it's very important to have clarity around your actual work and workflow and what causes confusion and stress when it is disrupted. These questions may help you identify an area where you might be able to set or maintain a boundary:

Is your reporting structure clear?

Is it clear who generates your assignments?

Who sets your work priorities?

From whom and how often do you receive feedback?

Do you treat others fairly without positive or negative feelings influencing your decisions?

Do others treat you fairly without positive or negative feelings influencing their decisions?

THINK

For most people, many of the following choices are automatic and not much conscious attention is paid to them. When setting and maintaining boundaries, it is helpful to become aware of the choices you make around your needs and see if your actions support what you need.

When do you arrive at and leave the office?

Do you accept meetings over lunch or breakfast?

Do you block time out for yourself to do your job?

Do you attend every meeting you are invited to?

Do you communicate your commitments/job responsibilities with others?

Do you ask questions when you have them?

Do you pick up the slack for others on your team?

Do you do tasks that are not part of your job description?

How often do you work from home?

Do you take vacation time?

Do you take personal time/breaks at work?

Do you have an "open door" policy?

DO

Answer the questions for yourself.

Share the questions with your team and family.

QUESTIONS TO CONSIDER

Describe your need for space — both physical and mental.

How much autonomy do you require?

What type of office behavior is unacceptable to you?

What are your current limits to how much work you can take on?

PRACTICE SUGGESTIONS

Set clear boundaries about when you come to work, when you take breaks, and how much you work from home.

Be consistent about the boundaries you set.

Keep your balance plan where you can see it.

Be open to changing your plan as your needs change.

Own all of your yes's and your no's.

PUT IT ALL TOGETHER

By now, you should have a clear idea of what balance means to you and have a baseline understanding of your behavior (values, actions, and words) and be able to recognize empowered and disempowered states of being. And now you have a solid direction on the boundaries you need to establish and enforce to set yourself up for success.

MAKE A PLAN

Develop a plan with five actions you are willing to take to create better alignment between your actions and your values over the next 30 days. For those of you who are stuck, try starting in the area where you feel most out of balance or where you think a change will make the most impact. Some examples for your plan might include the following:

Do one thing differently next week regarding how you spend your time.

Pick one value to work on honoring more.

Set one boundary.

Release some stress by getting physically active or improving your diet.

RESULT:
INDIVIDUAL BALANCE AGREEMENTS

ACTION 1

ACTION 3

ACTION 5

The five actions I am willing to take to create better alignment between my actions and values over the next 30 days are:

ACTION 2

ACTION 4

RESULT: TEAM BALANCE AGREEMENTS

INDIVIDUAL ACCOUNTABILITIES

Accept work-life balance is a choice

Accept delivering value to the company is a priority and at times will have impact on my balance

Push back on tasks with no tangible outcomes

Ask for assistance in prioritizing tasks

Feel empowered to leave work early/make more flexible arrangements during quieter periods

Communicate to my managers my work-life needs

Include work-life balance, simplification, and productivity goals in my commitments

Schedule activities important for balance

TEAM ACCOUNTABILITIES

Enhance personal productivity through improving time management

Seek out training as needed to improve skills

Meeting organizer schedules and runs meetings for maximum efficiency

Meeting attendees are fully present and engaged in meetings

Assume positive intent

AGREEMENTS UNIQUE TO TEAM:

Consider accountabilities for each role within a team and create your own team agreements to support balance.

MANAGER ACCOUNTABILITIES

Ensure that my team is fully aware of all company benefits that help with work-life balance

Ensure that my team members avail themselves of their full annual leave entitlement, and be flexible with requests

Help plan for coverage/re-allocation of work while employees are on vacation

Build and encourage team spirit and unified company attitude

Build in time for buffer or ad hoc work in commitments and recognize that extra work will emerge

Avoid setting expectations to perform work over weekends

Give as much advance notice as possible for situations that require special consideration

Print this charter and make it visible in my office

TEAM RESULTS

Established expectations and agreements around work-life balance

Established awareness around the impact of behavior on productivity and innovation

Empowerment to push back with professionalism and confidence

Improved team communication

Culture of authenticity

NOW WHAT?

When you are **ACCOUNTABLE, AUTHENTIC,** and **AWAKE** to your behavior (actions and words), it creates environments (in and outside of work) that allow you to be **INNOVATIVE** and **PRODUCTIVE.** When you feel innovative and productive in your environments, you create individual and organizational success that is sustainable.

YOU HOLD SO MUCH POWER RIGHT NOW. You have the opportunity to be in charge, to be empowered to create the life you want — a life that is different than repeating the past, a life that brings your actions in line with your values. A life created by you to match your individual needs for balance.

Because your needs for balance will change over time, you might find that, even with this knowledge, boundaries disappear, alignment between values and actions falls out of whack, or complaints come out as criticisms. THE MOST POWERFUL THING TO KNOW IS THAT YOU HAVE THE ABILITY AT ANY TIME TO STOP WHATEVER IT IS YOU ARE DOING AND THINK IT THROUGH — PAUSE AND USE YOUR AWARENESS SKILLS TO GET CLEAR ON WHAT IS CAUSING THE IMBALANCE YOU ARE FACING AND CREATE A PLAN TO TAKE ACTION.

BEST PRACTICES:
TIME

* Block out "think time" on your calendar each day (or at least once a week) to do your job (meaning no email or meetings in that time)

* Create on-ramp and off-ramp time in your day by blocking off the first and last 30 minutes to plan and revisit action items

* Be consistent with your calendar – it helps you plan your day and others plan around you

* Consolidate to one calendar with personal and professional activities combined for one view

* At the end of each day, write down the five things you need to do the next day to help your mind from wandering toward work throughout the night

* Set boundaries around when and how much you are going to work from home so others in your life can plan around and support your "office hours" (and be consistent about keeping the same hours)

* Say no to meetings that are not directly related to your work commitments

* Create "work-free" lunch time at least 2 days a week

* Resist the urge to be the first one to answer an email

* When emailing on weekends, state in your mail if you expect a response over the weekend

BEST PRACTICES:
TECHNOLOGY

* Be mindful of your IM status – do not allow people to contact you if you are in thinking or planning time

* Be mindful of how often you are doing work on your cell phone when not at work

* Be aware of where you charge your mobile device at night. (Does it have to be the bedroom, or will the kitchen work just as well?)

* Limit your social media time at work and think of it more as entertainment personal time

* Set a specific time (or times) each day to answer email so you are free to do your work the rest of the day

* Turn off your email alerts (or close Outlook) when you are working/planning so emails do not disturb you as they pop up on your desktop

BEST PRACTICES:
STRESS

* Get clear on what is causing you stress – is it a person, place, or situation?

* Take care of your body when you are feeling stress – the stress will keep coming unless resolved, so you will have to take care of it sooner or later

* Look for a solution to the things that stress you out – it might be that your attitude needs to shift

* Be present in the moment you are in – when your mind starts to wander, bring it back to the moment; simply say "no thank you" to your wandering thoughts when they occur

* Prioritize your values and commitments and spend more time on the ones higher on the list

BEST PRACTICES:
GENERAL

* Have a family meeting to share your values and boundaries

* Stop blaming other people for the things that are not going well in your life

* Accept responsibility for the choices you make

* Know what you are really complaining about – think before you share your dissatisfaction

* Complain with a solution attached to change the situation

* Say what you mean, and do what you say you are going to do

THE CHOICE IS YOURS.

ABOUT THE AUTHOR

After years in senior communication roles, working countless hours crafting content for executives at Microsoft, Jae collapsed from stress-related adrenal fatigue directly attributed to the way she was living her life. This life-altering experience propelled Jae deep into research on human behavior, neuro-science, mindfulness, and organizational relationship systems.

In 2008, Jae founded WLB Consulting Group and developed the Mindful Life Program, which includes four group coaching workshops to generate reflection, awareness, and action at the organizational and individual levels.

Jae has taught work-life awareness workshops to thousands of employees at Microsoft and other technology companies in more than 50 countries including China, Russia, India, Japan, Brazil, Argentina, United Arab Emirates, France, Germany, United Kingdom, Norway, Sweden, Canada, and the United States.

Jae has an extensive background in writing and communication with a master's degree in Communication Management from Colorado State University and a bachelor's degree in Broadcast Communication from Metropolitan State College of Denver. She holds certificates in co-active coaching and organizational relationship systems coaching and is the author of seven books.

OTHER BOOKS BY JAE ELLARD

The Five Truths about Work-life Balance is about moving past the misconceptions surrounding work, life, and balance.

The Pocket Coach: Perspective When You Need Some is a book of questions to help you make clear choices.

Success with Stress is about five proactive choices you can make to reduce stress.

THE MINDFUL LIFE COLLECTION

Stop & Think: Creating New Awareness is about the choices you have and the understanding of the impact of the choices you make.

Stop & See: Developing Intentional Habits is about your ability to consciously choose to create habits that support your definitions of balance and success.

Stop & Listen: Practicing Presence is about working with your choices to create deeper engagement with self, others and your environment.

Beyond Tips & Tricks: Mindful Management is about leading groups to take accountability for making and accepting choices.

Created by Jae Ellard
Edited by Jenifer Kooiman
Designed by Hannah Wygal & Big Fig Design, LLC

Stop & Think: Creating New Awareness, 1st edition
2011-2014 Copyright by Simple Intentions

ISBN 978-0-9828344-6-6

Simple Intentions is a conscious content company working to increase awareness in the
workplace. For more information please visit www.simpleintentions.com.